Nature's Super Secrets

What Makes Rain?

By Abby Wilson

Gareth Stevens
Publishing

Please visit our website, www.garethstevens.com. For a free color catalog of all our high-quality books, call toll free 1-800-542-2595 or fax 1-877-542-2596.

Library of Congress Cataloging-in-Publication Data

Wilson, Abby
     What makes rain? / by Abby Wilson.
   cm. – (Nature's super secrets)
   Includes bibliographical references and index.
   Summary: Brief text and photographs describe how rain forms and tell about the water cycle.
   Contents: Rain, rain, go away – Why does it rain? – Inside the clouds – Rainy day.
   ISBN 978-1-4339-8171-5 (pbk.)
   ISBN 978-1-4339-8172-2 (6-pack)
   ISBN 978-1-4339-8170-8 (hard bound)
   1. Rain and rainfall—Juvenile literature   2. Hydrologic cycle—Juvenile
literature   [1. Rain and rainfall   2. Hydrologic cycle]   I. Title
            2013
      551.57/7—dc23

Published in 2013 by
Gareth Stevens Publishing
111 East 14th Street, Suite 349
New York, NY 10003

Copyright © 2013 Gareth Stevens Publishing

Designer: Nicholas Domiano
Editor: Sarah Machajewski

Photo credits: Cover Galyna Andrushko/Shutterstock.com; p. 5 Lane V. Erickson/Shutterstock.com; p. 7 Zsolt. Biczó/Shutterstock.com; p. 9 Nacivet/Photographer's Choice/Getty Images; p. 11 Serp/Shutterstock.com; p. 13 Jake Sorensen/Shutterstock.com; p. 15 Fedorov Oleksiy/Shutterstock.com; p. 17 Serg64/Shutterstock.com;   p. 17 Plus69/Shutterstock.com; p. 19 Andrew Chin/Shutterstock.com;   p. 21 Michele Rosenthal/Flickr/Getty Images

Printed in the United States of America

CPSIA compliance information: Batch #CW13GS: For further information contact Gareth Stevens, New York, New York at 1-800-542-2595.

Contents

Rain, Rain, Go Away 4

Why Does It Rain? 8

Inside the Clouds. 12

Rainy Day. 18

Glossary. 22

For More Information. 23

Index 24

Boldface words appear in the glossary.

Rain, Rain, Go Away

You may feel sad when it rains, since it means you have to play inside. But rain is a good thing! Rain gives us water, which is the most important thing on Earth. Earth needs water for many reasons.

All living things need water to stay alive. Rain gives us water to drink and helps our plants grow. It makes lakes and rivers, and keeps the oceans deep. It also cools us off when it's hot.

Why Does It Rain?

All our water has been around since Earth was young. It moves in something called the water **cycle**. The water cycle shows us the different forms water takes. Rain is one step of the water cycle.

9

Rain comes from the water in our lakes, oceans, and rivers. The sun shines down on the water and makes it **evaporate**. Water evaporates in the form of **vapor**. The vapor goes into the air and rises to form clouds.

Inside the Clouds

When the vapor gets very high, it turns back into tiny water droplets. This happens because the air is cooler. Clouds collect thousands of droplets that turn into rain. Clouds get bigger as more vapor rises.

13

The **temperature** of the air helps make rain, too. When warm air and cold air meet, warm air pushes cold air into the sky. Cold air makes clouds bigger. It also pushes the droplets together to make rain.

15

The inside of a cloud is very cold. It even holds little pieces of ice! The ice mixes with water and makes the raindrops big and heavy. The raindrops wait in the clouds until it's time to rain.

Rainy Day

When the clouds can't hold any more water, it rains! Sometimes it only rains for a few minutes. Other times, it rains all day. When it rains a lot, it sounds really loud. Do you know what rain sounds like?

Every part of the world needs water. Some places need a lot of rain. It can rain every day in the rainforest. Deserts only get a little rain. They're very dry. Does it rain a lot where you live?

What Happens to Water?

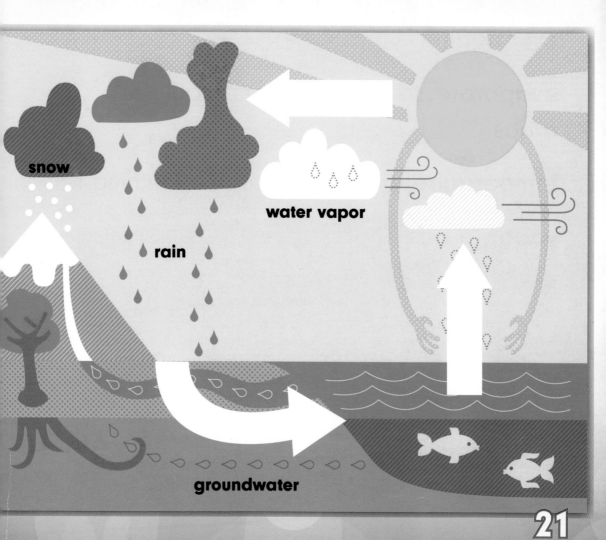

snow

rain

water vapor

groundwater

Glossary

cycle: a set of steps that happen over and over again

evaporate: to change from a liquid to a gas

temperature: how hot or cold something is

vapor: a gas

For More Information

Books

Jango-Cohen, Judith. *Why Does It Rain?* Minneapolis, MN: Millbrook Press, 2006.

Sherman, Josepha. *Splish! Splash! A Book About Rain.* Bloomington, MN: Picture Window Books, 2004.

Websites

Precipitation

www.kidsgeo.com/geography-for-kids/0111-precipitation.php
Read about the science of rain and where it comes from.

The Water Cycle

www.kidzone.ws/water/
Learn every step of the water cycle with fun pictures and examples.

Publisher's note to educators and parents: Our editors have carefully reviewed these websites to ensure that they are suitable for students. Many websites change frequently, however, and we cannot guarantee that a site's future contents will continue to meet our high standards of quality and educational value. Be advised that students should be closely supervised whenever they access the Internet.

Index

air 10, 12, 14

clouds 10, 12, 14, 16, 18

desert 20

droplets 12, 14

evaporate 10

ice 16

lakes 6, 10

oceans 6, 10

raindrops 16

rainforest 20

rivers 6, 10

vapor 10, 12

water cycle 8